Secrets to Creating a Successful Business

Secrets to Creating a Successful Business

Written by: Becky Vannes

Published by Oracle Publishing

Publication Year: 2018

First Printing: 2018

ISBN 978-0-578-41327-3

Oracle Publishing
9140 Topneck St.
New Port Richey, FL 34654

www.oraclespublishing.com

Table of Contents

DISCLAIMER

The information contained in this book is for general guidance on matters of interest only. The application and impact of strategies, theories and laws can vary widely based on the specific facts involved. Given the changing nature of market forces, laws, rules and regulations, and the inherent hazards of communication, there may be delays, omissions or inaccuracies in information contained herein.

Accordingly, the information in this book is provided with the understanding that the authors and publishers are not herein engaged in rendering legal, accounting, tax, corporate finance, investment, banking, or other professional advice and/or services. As such, it should not be used as a substitute for consultation with professional accounting, tax, legal, corporate finance, investment, banking, or other competent advisors.

Before making any decision or taking any action, you should consult a professional advisor. While we have made every attempt to ensure that the information contained in this book is reliable, MBVPRO LLC is not responsible for any errors or omissions, or for the results obtained from the use of this information. All information in this book is provided with no guarantee of completeness, accuracy, timeliness or of the results obtained from the use of this information, and without warranty of any kind, expressed or implied, including, but not limited to warranties of performance, merchantability for a particular purpose.

In no event will MBVPRO LLC, its related partnerships, corporations or other entities, or the partners, agents or employees thereof be liable to you or anyone else for any decision made or action taken in reliance on the information in this book or for any consequential, special or similar damages, even if advised of the possibility of such damages.

Certain information in this book may have come from other sources (including websites) created and/or maintained by partnerships, corporations or other entities related to MBVPRO LLC or by third parties unrelated to MBVPRO LLC. MBVPRO LLC makes no representations as to the accuracy or any other aspect of this information.

Letter to The Reader

Dear Friend,

Congratulations and welcome! The next 5 days you will begin a journey towards creating a business that will not only help you to achieve the financial freedom you want and deserve, and assist with your creative process, but also to change the lives of the people you will serve.

Over the past decade I have been literally obsessed with how businesses (both online and offline) generate and monetize customers, as well as the creative process of business. While learning and applying these methods in my own businesses, as well as hundreds of others around the world, I have developed a process that we've used countless times to break down the creation of a business into 5 simple steps, to double the traffic, conversions and sales for almost any product or service online.

I'm truly excited and privileged to have this opportunity to share with you the best of what I have learned. Enjoy this program, but more importantly, USE IT!

Thanks,

Becky Vannes

How to Use this Book

Before we even get started can we take a second to acknowledge what you've chosen by purchasing and reading this book. If you've picked up this book it probably means that you are ready to make a new demand for you and your business to be greater.

Each chapter has its own theme and sets of questions to aid you in getting clear about what your business currently is and where you'd like to take it. As you begin to go through the workbook to answer questions please recognize there is no right or wrong answers.

These questions are to gain awareness on what is stopping you and getting you to a place where you stop judging you so you can begin to create your life and business.

Would you be willing to be honest with you? You might right down the first answer that comes to mind and then you can always revisit them again later. This workbook can continue to add to your business each time you go through so you might consider coping the page, but I would recommend writing your answers and keeping them as a tool to for you to see your progress.

It was designed to be a quick five-day jumpstart program and I invite you to take as much time as you need. If you choose to do it, you choose to do it and if not that's okay too. Don't make this a struggle or obstacle for you.

Would you be willing to be honest with you? You might right down the first answer that comes to mind and then you can always revisit them again later.

What if you could have fun with it? What if you gave yourself permission to play with your business? What if the only thing your business required to create something greater than you have now is for you to enjoy it?

Are you ready to give it a try? What do you have to lose?

BUSINESS ENTITY CREATION

Business

Educate yourself about setting up a business in your country and region. What are the laws and regulations? Find the local business support services for your area.

In the USA, there are Small Business Development Centers that offer services to small businesses. There are similar organization in European countries. Do an internet search on phrases like "small business support", "starting a business in a Santa Fe County (enter your city)", etc., to find local resources for your area.

Business Entity

Business name - what are you calling your business? Do an internet search to see who else might be using the same business name.

Type of legal entity - what type of legal entity will work for you and your business? For example, in the USA there's Sole-proprietorship, LLC, S-Corporation, etc.... Research the types of businesses in your country and what's going to work for you.

Taxes and Licenses - what business licenses, tax registrations, etc. are required in your area? For my LLC in the USA I filed articles of organization with my state Regulation Commission, applied for a Federal Tax Identification number, a state tax Identification number, and a county business license.

Business Finances

Keeping separate personal and business accounts (banking, credit/debit card etc.) can make tracking your business finances easier and may be required for your business entity.

Financial records and filing taxes - create a system that works for you for tracking your business income, expenses, receipts and for producing the reports you need for taxes. Know what taxes you are required to pay and when. They will be called different things in different countries but there is likely to be some sort of sales or VAT tax, service tax, income tax, or something else?

DAY 1: Getting Clear on Products & Targets

First thing is YOU are your business and YOU are your product. Your clients will choose you because of who you are and what you have to offer. People crave the energy and gift that you are to them and whatever area of their life they are looking to change.

Now if you heard that and started to judge yourself or question yourself, keep reading , and if you take your time to complete this chapter honestly you will realize that what you have to offer really is special, even if you don't believe it. Remember you are always the hardest on yourself.

Now, let's take a look at what you have, what you'd like to have and what it is going to take to get you there.

GETTING CLEAR ON YOUR PRODUCT AND YOUR BUSINESS TARGET

What is Your Product?

_____

_____

_____

Who is Your Dream Customer?

_____

_____

_____

Where Are Your Dream Customers?

_____

_____

_____

_____

What Marketing Are You Going to Use to Attract Them?

_____

_____

_____

_____

Where Are You Going to Take Them?

_____

_____

_____

_____

WHAT IS THE LEAST AMOUNT OF WORK YOU NEED TO DO TO REACH YOUR GOALS?

What Amount of Money Would You Like to Create? ($ Amount)

_____

_____

What is the Maximum Amount of Money You've Decided You Can

Create? ($ Amount)

_____

_____

What is the Monthly Costs to Create Your Life AND Business?

_____

_____

How Much Money Do You Require Per Month to Live and Run Your

Business?

_____

_____

_____

How Many Sales Per Month Do You Need to Hit That Goal?

_____

_____

_____

DAY 2: Website & Facebook Business Page/Groups

Your website homepage is your commercial to hook your customers, the average page view before they click off is 20- 60 seconds. Think of your home page as your quick infomercial to sell you and your product. Your website is where people find you and get to know who you are.

Another great tool to use is a Facebook Business Page. Having a business page is a quick way to invite people to interact with you, share your information and being seen. It is important for this not to only be about selling a product, but building a connection with potential clients.

Combining these two systems allows you to show how you live and be your product. It is an opportunity to show the world who you are and what you'd like to invite them too.

For this chapter, look at these questions from the eyes of a new client. I wonder what you can discover about the information you have shared and what you can now be aware of?

WEBSITE

Go to your website and answer the questions below. Does your website contribute to addressing them?

What Is Your Story? Who Are You and Why Should I Choose You?

_____

_____

_____

_____

_____

_____

_____

What Are You Inviting Them To?

_____

_____

_____

_____

_____

_____

What Is Your Product Your Selling on The Homepage...? Is It Clear?

_____

_____

_____

_____

_____

What Do You Desire to Create as Your Business with Your Website?

_____

_____

_____

_____

_____

How Can You Best Serve Your Dream Client?

_____

_____

_____

_____

_____

How Can You Provide Monthly Value to Your Client?

_____

_____

_____

_____

_____

_____

Do you have an email sign up for your list? Are You Offering Them
an Incentive to Sign Up for Your Email List? (Free eBook, Free
Membership Group, etc.)

_____

_____

_____

_____

_____

FACEBOOK BUSINESS PAGE

What Is Your Main Message on Your Business Page? Go Right to
The Beginning and Look at It Like a Viewer Would?

_____

_____

_____

_____

_____

Is Your FB Business Page All Promotions or Are You Adding Fun
Non-Selling Posts?

_____

_____

_____

Search for Events and Pages That Are in Your Niche. Where Do Your
Best Clients Connect and What Are They Talking About?

_____

_____

_____

_____

Pay Attention to Who Is in Your Niche and Who Is Earning Money?

_____

_____

_____

DAY 3: Everything Back-End Systems

The target for a backend system should be to have an easy flow of engagement from purchase to delivery (live call, downloadable product, eCourses, etc....) They allow you to stay involved in the creative process, while maintaining a connection to your clients.

While your website shares your why and gets your business in front of potential clients, your backend systems are what you'd like people to be able to do once they find you. With this home play, we will look at possible systems you might require so you can consider the feature when choosing a website hosting platform such as Wix, WordPress or Weebly.

What Would You Like People to Be Able to Do on Your Website? What Systems Are Required for Your Clients to Successfully Complete Those Tasks?

_____

_____

_____

_____

_____

_____

_____

Does Your Website Have a Store or Live Events Calendar Where Clients Can Register and Pay in One or Few Steps?

_____

_____

Does Your Website Have a Built-In System for Accepting Payments? What Is Your Preferred Way for People to Pay?

_____

_____

_____

Does Your Website Have a Built-In System for Emailing Marketing, Purchase Emails or Order Confirmations?

_____

_____

_____

What Systems Can You Use That Allow You to Have Fun, Feel Confident and Stay in Creation? Do You Desire to Run the Systems? Do You Need to Hire Someone? Are You Intimidated by Systems?

_____

_____

_____

_____

Who Do You Know That Has Brilliant Systems? What Do You Enjoy or Not Enjoy About Their Systems?

_____

_____

_____

_____

_____

_____

Do Your Current Systems, Or Future Systems, Allow Your Clients to Easily Engage, Interact, and Appear Connected to You on A Personal Level?

_____

_____

_____

_____

_____

_____

RECOMMENDATIONS FOR BACKEND SYSTEMS

Websites:

Wix www.wix.com

Weebly www.weebly.com (Weebly is more cost effective, but contains less integrated systems than Wix)

WordPress www.wordpress.com (WordPress requires some knowledge of coding and updates often)

Payment Systems:

PayPal www.paypal.com

Square www.Square.com

Email Marketing:

Mail Chimp www.mailchimp.com

Constant Contact www.ConstantContact.com

Online Conference Lines:

www.FreeConferenceCallHD.com

www.InstantTeleseminar.com

Web Conference:

Zoom- www.Zoom.us

UberConference www.uberconference.com/

Collaborative Systems: (all have both free and paid plans)

Skype www.skype.com

Slack www.slack.com

Google Drive drive.google.com

Management Organization Systems

Asana www.asana.com

Trello www.trello.com

Basecamp www.basecamp.com

Online Storage Systems: (all have both free and paid plans)

Drobox www.dropbox.com

Google Drive drive.google.com

Hightail www.hightail.com

Box www.box.com

EMAIL TEMPLATES

The following are email template examples that you can edit and use for your own classes and products. Feel free to make any edits or use these templates as inspiration for you to get started. Be sure at the end of each email you have a UNSUBSCRIBE button and explanation of how you use people's information in marketing in order to follow the new Data Protection Laws. I recommend doing your own research on this matter to ensure total compliance with the regulations.

Telecall Auto-Responder

Thank you so much for choosing more and registering for the *[Insert Call Name]* Telecall!

This series is from *[Insert Dates and Times]*.

There will be *[Insert #]* calls on *[Insert # and Different Topics/Topic Name]*.

Please be sure to pay for these calls before they begin to ensure you receive the call-in detail emails!

Click **HERE** *[Insert Link/s Here]* to pay by credit card, or by PayPal via *[Insert Link/Email]*. These calls are *[Insert Price and Currency]*.

I look forward to having you on the series!

Upcoming calls

Call 1 - DATE/TIME

Your Time in the World: *[Insert Link - Using Website TimeAndDate.Com]*

Call 2 - DATE/TIME

Your Time in the World: *[Insert Link - Using Website TimeAndDate.Com]*

Call 3 - DATE/TIME

Your Time in the World: *[Insert Link - Using Website TimeAndDate.Com]*

If you have any questions about your payments for this class, please email me at *[Insert Email Address]*.

NOTE: If you are paying with a non-US credit card - This transaction will be run through a US bank account. Please note that you may incur international bank fees if you are not using a US credit card. (if this applies to you/your country)

Telecall Payment Reminder

Dear *[Insert Client's Name or Merge Tag]*,

The *[Insert Name of Call]* call starts in *[Insert # of Days]* days. Will you be joining us?

We have received your registration. You just have one more step!

For ease the payment details are below. Call topics, dates and times follow!

HERE ARE YOUR PAYMENT OPTIONS:

You can pay via PayPal by making a payment to *[Insert Link/Email].*

*** If you have already paid and you still received this email, please let us know and we will check our records again.

[Insert Call Details, # of Days and Prices]

Once we receive your payment you will be sent the call-in details for this teleseries via email.

*** Please note: if we do not receive your payment 24 hours before the call, we cannot not guarantee that you will receive the call-in details in time for the start of the 1st call. ***It takes 24 hours to process and document the payment.*** We really appreciate your contribution by submitting your payment early.

This series includes:

- **3** x 60-90 minute calls *[Adjust This for Your Emails]*

Call 1 Date, Time - Title/Description

[Insert Link - Using Website TimeAndDate.Com]

Call 2 Date, Time - Title/Description

[Insert Link - Using Website TimeAndDate.Com]

Call 3 Date, Time - Title/Description

[Insert Link - Using Website TimeAndDate.Com]

DAY 4: Social Media Marketing

The way people communicate is changing in a big way. With social media marketing think of yourself as a social engineer. You need to return to the basics of marketing. If you want people to click on your posts/ads, you need to figure out what they're struggling with or what they're trying to make progress on. Figure out creative ways to engage with your client. Focus on your audience and what's important to them. Try to drive relationships as well as engagement.

One of the best ways to engage your audience is by providing them with a compelling reason to share your message with their networks in a way that is natural and seamless. Word-of-mouth marketing and peer recommendations are an extremely powerful way to increase brand visibility through social posts as people believe their network of peers more often than a brand running an ad.

What Does It Take to Do Social Media Marketing Well? What Have You Decided This Is?

_____

_____

_____

_____

What Are Your Social Media Marketing Strategy Goals?

_____

_____

_____

Do You Belong to Any Facebook Groups?

_____

_____

_____

_____

Are You Active or Engaging in Facebook Groups? Do You Ask
Questions or Just Sell? What Can You Add or Give to The Group
Members to Invite Them to Your Business and Products?

_____

_____

_____

_____

What's Going on In Your Audience's Lives?

_____

_____

_____

_____

What Are They (Potential Clients) Trying to Do?

_____

_____

_____

_____

_____

What Could You Do to Give Them Forward Progress? And Can You Use This as Inspiration to Craft Your Post, Live Videos, Ads, And Messenger Marketing?

_____

_____

_____

_____

Engaging Using Your Business Page

Have You Scheduled Posts on Your Business Page? This Is a Great Way to Keep Your Business Page Active.

_____

_____

_____

Have You Done a Facebook Live? Live and Be Your Product. Talk About You and How Your Life Has Changed Because Of What You Have Done. This Is Being Your Product.

_____

_____

_____

Have You Done a Facebook Event with Your Business Page? You Have the Tools to Boost Your Events as well as See the Analytics of Your Events.

_____

_____

_____

_____

Do You Add Your Website Link to Every Post That Talks About an Event or Product?

_____

_____

_____

_____

FACEBOOK PIXEL

The Facebook Pixel is an analytics tool that allows you to measure the effectiveness of your advertising by understanding the actions people take on your website. You can use Pixel data to:

- Make sure your ads are being shown to the right people
- Build advertising audiences
- Unlock additional Facebook advertising tools

You can set up the Facebook pixel by placing pixel code on the header of your website. When someone visits your website, and takes an action (like completing a purchase), the Facebook pixel is triggered and reports this action. This way, you'll know when a customer takes an action, and will be able to reach that customer again through future Facebook ads. Pixel ads track your customers and give you data on whether your ads are effective.

Benefits

With the Facebook pixel, you can:

- Find new customers, or people who have visited a specific page or taken a desired action on your website.
- Create lookalike audiences to reach more people who are similar to your best customers.
- Drive more sales.
- Measure the results of your ads.

Before You Begin

- You'll need a website for your business.
- You must be able to update your website's code.

Create a Facebook Pixel

- Go to your Pixels tab in Events Manager.
  https://www.facebook.com/events_manager/pixel/events
- Click Create a Pixel.

Add the Facebook Pixel to your website

Once you've created your pixel, you're ready to put the Facebook pixel code on your website. Research your website for how to add a pixel code.

Your Facebook events manager link above has step by step articles on how to set up your ads.

INSTAGRAM

To gain more followers on Instagram is the goal for business marketing. One way to gain followers is to search for common hashtags. A second way is to follow people in similar niches, as well as follow people who have followed them. Best practice is to also follow individuals and businesses who follow you.

To get a larger reach, be sure to make your account a business account and connect it to your Facebook business page. Instagram and Facebook are now connected and if you are running ads on Facebook you can connected and run them on Instagram.

Search the trending hashtags and use them in your captions. Add hashtags that will reach the people your post is most related to.

Question Stickers

The Questions Sticker allows you to ask your followers any question that you'd like. Users who view the story can reply to the questions, and you'll be able to see all their responses privately.

If you choose, you can share these responses publicly within the Stories feed, so this is a great way to start a conversation and gather social proof all at once.

Linktree

Linktree can help you get more out of the single link you add to your Instagram bio. Instagram also does not allow links in the description of your pictures. Linktree allows you to add several links to one. This allows you to run several ads and allow everyone to find the ads they are following/purchasing.

DAY 5: GO TIME!

This chapter is the chapter in this book where we talk about your goals, your dreams, and how to get more of whatever you want and make more money.

I call this concept GO TIME because it's all about taking action right now, TODAY. It's not called "Wait." It's not called "Maybe Later." It's not called "Pause and worry and ruminate for the next six months." It is called GO TIME!

What if you already have everything you require? Why wait?

WOULD YOU LIKE TO MAKE MORE MONEY?

I have a challenge today to help you with that. Whether you want to get more clients, start the new business, add to your business, pay off your debt, travel the world, you're going to need money. And when we have more money, we have more power, so it's one of my favorite things to develop with entrepreneurs.

Money amplifies your voice. Money allows you to reach farther and serve even more people. Money makes things happen. Money gets things done. Money is a big form of power and potency.

I want you to have all the power that you can possibly have. Please don't shy away from this power. Embrace it. Harness it. Use it to do wonderful things.

Would You Like to Make More Money?

_____

_____

_____

What Does Making More Money Mean to You?

_____

_____

_____

_____

_____

How Would Money Change Your Life?

_____

_____

_____

_____

_____

What Does Making More Money Mean to Your Business?

_____

_____

_____

_____

_____

It's very important to understand what having more money in your life would create for you. You want the things that you want, whether it's more money, more media coverage, more influence, or something else completely. When you understand WHAT the money will create for you, it energizes you, it clarifies your next steps, and it helps you really commit to your targets and stick with it. Let's find out.

How Much Money Would You Like to Earn in The Upcoming Year?

_____

_____

Write Down One Idea on How You Could Create That Number?

_____

_____

_____

What Could You Do to Earn or Create That Money? Do You Need to Launch a New Product? Do You Need to Raise Your Hourly Rate By 20%? What Do You Require and What is Your Business Asking For?

_____

_____

_____

_____

_____

ASKING FOR THE SALE

You might be thinking, "Well, I don't run a business yet, so this doesn't apply to me." But actually, this conversation applies to EVERYONE.

Because we're all selling "something." You might want to sell…a session, an eBook, a service. You might want to sell a house. You might want to sell an item or a call. You might want to sell tickets to an event. You might want to sell your skills to a new employer and get hired. You might want to sell an idea, a plan, a vision to your team at work…

Selling doesn't necessarily mean that you're selling a product. Selling means that you're DESCRIBING something with enthusiasm… and then you're INVITING people to say "YES" to whatever you're proposing.

Everyone needs to learn how to sell with confidence—regardless of whether you run a business or not.

You've probably describe things you were super excited about and never thought twice about. You didn't feel awkward or weird about it, right? You felt excited! You felt enthusiastic! You felt thrilled to share the information!

That's how sales should feel… all the time. That's the kind of energy you want to tap into.

Whatever you're selling—whether it's a product, a service, an idea, a proposition—when you're selling it, it should feel like you're texting your friend to describe the most AMAZING exciting sale.

Are You Excited About Your Product? Name One Thing That Is Exciting About Your Product!

_____

_____

Would You Have to Change Anything in Your Life, Business or Product to Get Excited About the Sale?

_____

_____

_____

What Can You Share Today on Your Social Media About You, Your Life and Your Product with That Excitement?

_____

_____

_____

_____

What Can You Start Implementing to Be Your Product Daily and Share Your Enthusiasm About Your Life? This Is a Soft Sell Being Your Product.

_____

_____

_____

I want to inspire _____ to say YES to:

_____

_____

Just One Step...

We have come to the end of these 5 days. The one thing I would like to say to wrap it all up is... Just take one step!

If the phone isn't ringing today, just take one step.

If your inbox isn't full of client inquiries today, just take one step...

If you're feeling invisible, feeling like nobody knows you exist, just take one step...

One step doesn't mean sit on the couch and wait for a big break...

Just take one step, doesn't mean dawdle around being busy, looking busy...

Just take one step means take action and institute something. Take whatever resources you currently have and do something to improve your situation. This might mean taking a class—or teaching one. It might mean blasting out a newsletter, sending a press release, or starting your own podcast. It might mean reading a book—or writing one. Most likely it just takes one step you have been avoiding.

Before you quit, see what happens when you take *just one step*.

With Gratitude,

Becky Vannes

Acknowledgements

I would like to acknowledge my mom and dad for always being the wind beneath my wings!

My husband for always inspiring me to be better and to just take one more step.

Luciana Ramsey who taught me that true success is having the discipline to do what you know you should do, even when you don't feel like doing it.

John Wheeler for having my back during the production of this workbook and being willing to contribute to my life, living and business in more ways than one.

Lastly, I want to thank all of you, the readers, for being willing to trust in me to gift you these amazing tools and for continuously seeing the opportunity to create something greater.